T0037756

This book is dedicated to my momma,
who believed in me long before I believed in myself.

www.FlowerpotPress.com
DJS-1010-0203
ISBN: 978-1-4867-1871-9
Made in China/Fabriqué en Chine

CULTURED D🍩NUTS

TAKE A BITE OUT OF ART HISTORY

BY CHLOE TYLER

What's on the menu?
TABLE OF CONTENTS

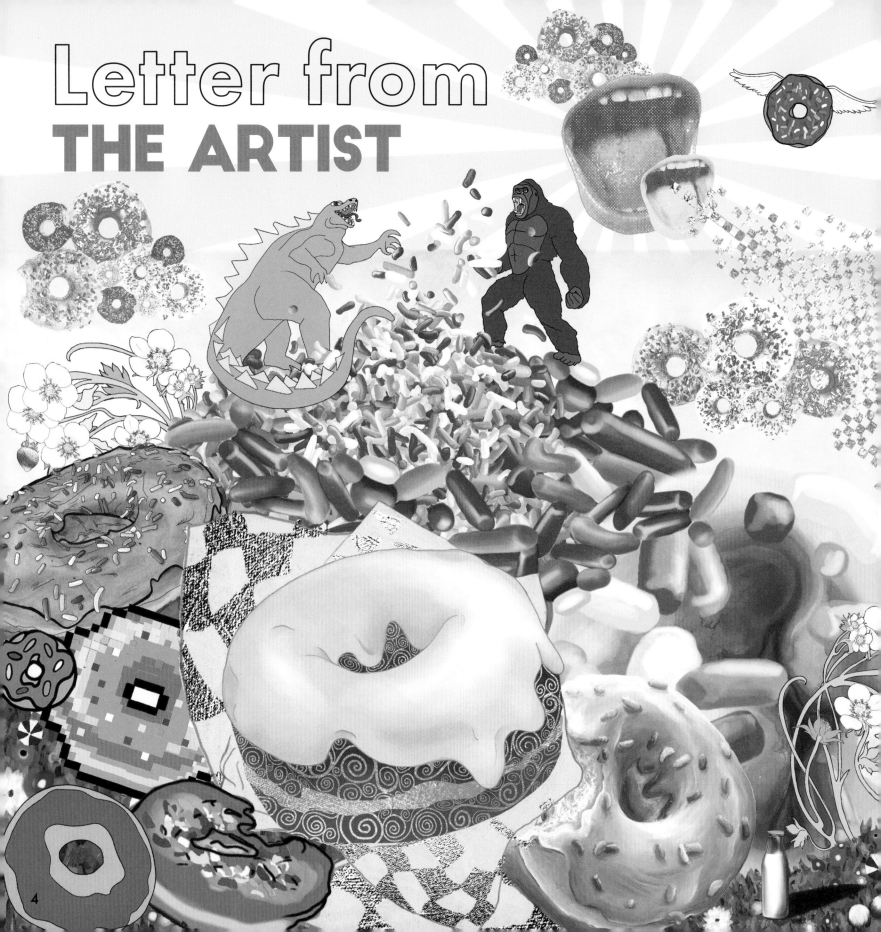

Letter from
THE ARTIST

In this book you will find works created by some of the greatest artists in history, works I created to emulate these artists, and a lot of donuts. Why? Well, I'm a believer in learning from the greatest to become one of the greatest. Why donuts? Let's just say I have a sweet tooth that is impossible to satisfy and donuts are often on my mind. Mix these ideas together, put some sprinkles on top, and BOOM, *Cultured Donuts* is born ... three years later. Turns out it's not easy imitating the best—not easy at all! After countless hours of drawing, painting, splattering, and even sculpting donuts (none of which are featured because, incidentally, sculpting is not my forte), I am thrilled to say mission accomplished. (Let's ignore the fact that Michelangelo painted the ENTIRE Sistine Chapel in just FOUR years, woah!)

Each donut in this book emulates the style of a different artist, from da Vinci and Michelangelo all the way to Yokoo and Basquiat. These donuts show how artists are influenced by those who came before and how each pushed the boundaries of the art world into new realms of possibility for future artists.

Every artist throughout history is connected because they all learn from and inspire each other. These individuals made such an impact while they were alive that their influence has lived on forever. It was only after seeing the radical works of Monet's Impressionist paintings that Seurat would study the science behind light and color and create pointillism. Pollock might never have reached the fame he achieved if not for his friend and fellow artist Willem de Kooning pushing him out of his comfort zone and into the painting (literally). My favorite artist, Egon Schiele, may have never picked up a brush if Klimt hadn't agreed to be his lifelong mentor the day he showed up at Klimt's studio. One painter influences the next, and they all mimic each other until they have the experience, skill, and inspiration to create something great on their own.

I hope these donuts help you recognize the specific aesthetics that define each artist. These aesthetics have shaped (and will continue to shape) the art world. Maybe these styles will influence your own art one day! Imitating the techniques of each artist in this book has profoundly shaped my own hand. I find myself curving my brushstrokes into swirling patterns like van Gogh, finding inspiration in the things that colored my childhood like Yokoo, and pushing myself to be bolder like Basquiat. Sometimes I'll even leave tiny pieces of debris in my paintings like Pollock. Unlike many of these artists, I have access to modern technologies that have allowed me to create and explore more freely. As you'll see, I try to utilize this advantage as much as possible.

This book is a little artifact of my journey as an artist attempting to echo artists I admire and aspire to be. Although completing this three-year-long study was a painstaking process, it has led me into a season of life where I feel more confident than ever in my abilities and ideas. More importantly, it has given me the honest experience and skill to support that mindset. I hope you all can learn something from it too!

— Chloe Tyler

Da Vinci Donut (1452 – 1519)

Born near the Italian town of Vinci in 1452, Leonardo da Vinci's name translates as Leonardo from the town of Vinci, so anyone who knows his name, and knows Italian, already knows where he is from. Leonardo was born during the Renaissance, a time of great discovery and rediscovery in art, science, and literature.

At the age of 14, he was sent to apprentice with a renowned artist named Andrea del Verrocchio. He would spend the rest of his life painting, sculpting, imagining, and inventing all kinds of wonderful works. Beyond art, da Vinci was also very interested in engineering, architecture, anatomy, and more. All these areas of interest informed and impacted each other significantly.

Da Vinci was considered a master of chiaroscuro, a method that uses stark contrasts to create the illusion of light in his paintings. He was also a prolific draftsman and kept many journals and sketches. Some of his most famous works are his technical and scientific drawings that relied on observing and understanding a subject matter in a deep and detailed way. He even drew a number of inventions that were so advanced that it would be hundreds of years before they could be built and tested.

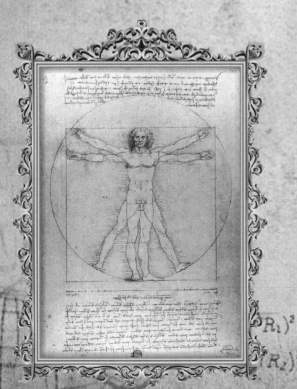

Delicious Detail

Many of his notes and writings were done using mirror writing. There are different opinions as to why he did this, but it may have been as simple as wanting a neat page. Using ink was a bit messier back then and da Vinci was left-handed, so writing in reverse—from right to left—kept his notes from getting smudged.

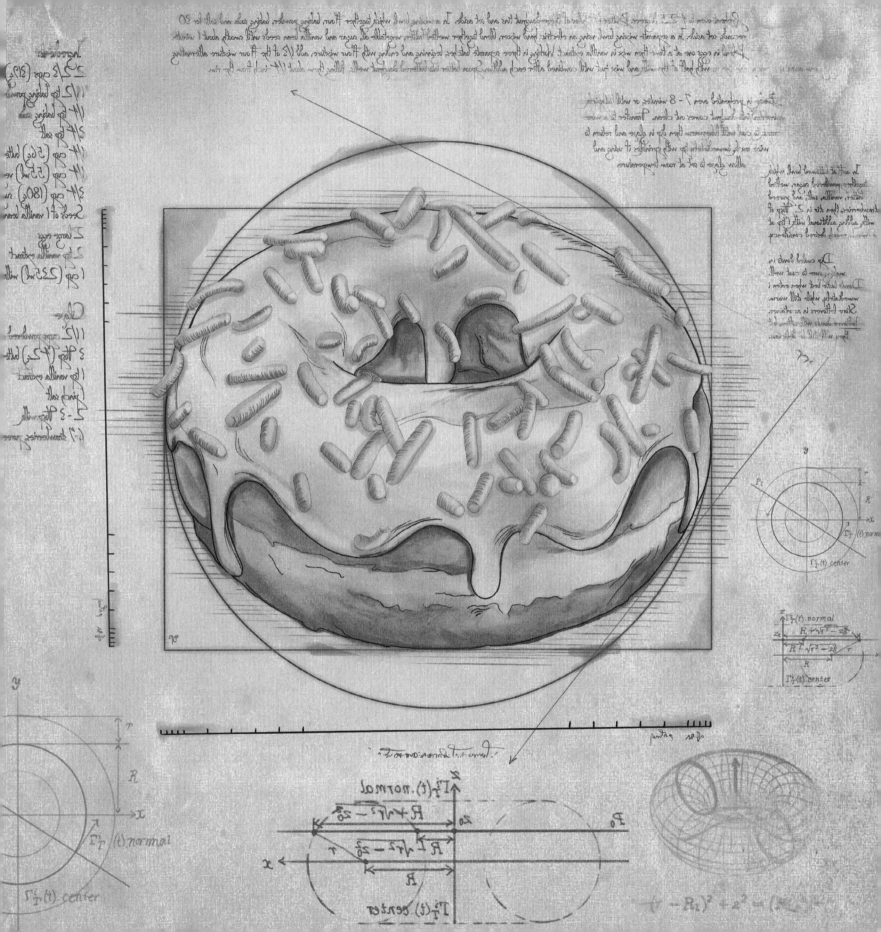

Michelangelo Donut (1475–1564)

Michelangelo di Lodovico Buonarroti Simoni was a Renaissance sculptor and painter born in 1475 in Caprese, Italy. Michelangelo was and still is considered one of the most accomplished artists of all time. He is most famously known for his spectacular frescoes painted on the ceiling of the Sistine Chapel.

He was born into a family that had once been Italian nobility. Against his father's wishes, he began his career as an artist when he started his apprenticeship at the age of 13. After a year, he left and began to pursue sculpture, going on to create famous marble sculptures such as the *Bacchus* and the *David*, both of which are located in the cultural hub of Florence, where Michelangelo trained to become an artist.

The objects and subjects in his paintings have a shape and volume that seem to jump from his art. His painting style created contrast through light and shadow and combined a harmony of bright and airy colors to give much of his work a heavenly glow.

Delicious Detail

Michelangelo rarely signed his work and didn't create any formal self-portraits, but he did hide himself in some of his sculptures and paintings. His likeness is said to be in a number of his works, including on the ceiling of the Sistine Chapel.

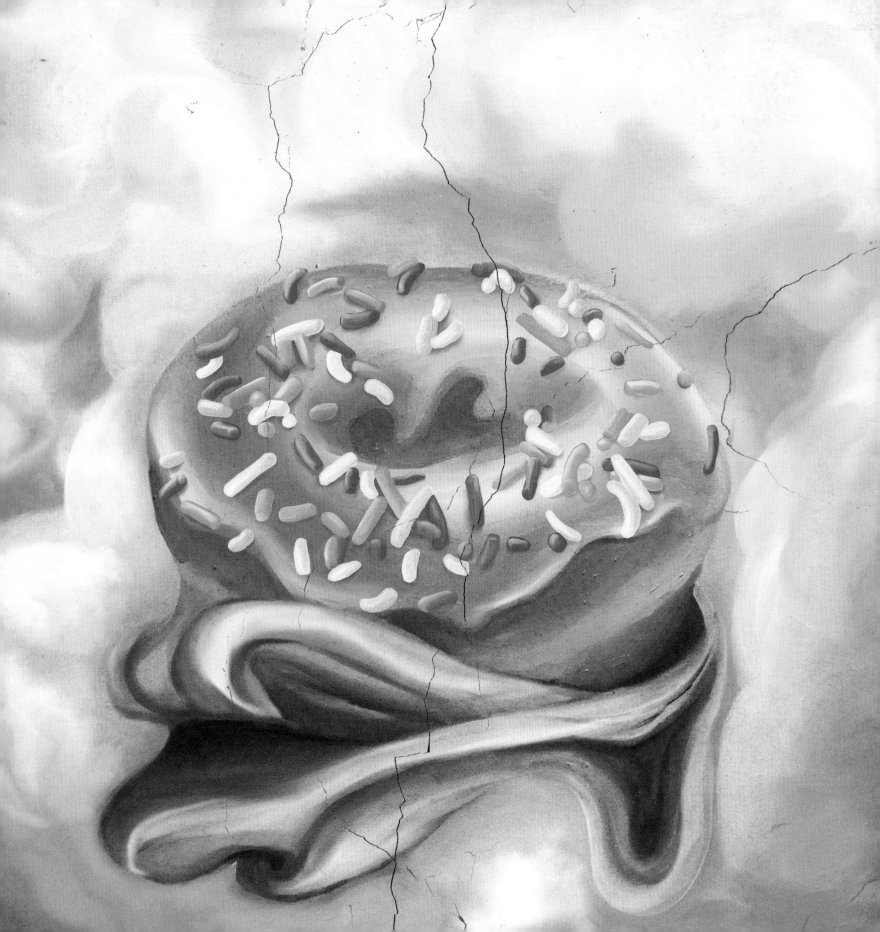

Rembrandt Donut (1606–1669)

Rembrandt van Rijn was born in 1606 in Leiden, Netherlands. He was an artist of the Dutch Golden Age and known for his incredible portraits. Some historians even say he was notorious for finding beauty in unconventionally beautiful people and things.

Born as the youngest son of ten children, he had no plans to follow in his father's footsteps and become a miller. Shortly after enrolling at the University of Leiden, he began to study painting which led to an extremely successful career as an artist.

Although his paintings have earned him much acclaim, his drawings are almost equally well-known. Within his drawings he explored lighting extensively and even created a portrait lighting technique, known as Rembrandt lighting, that is still used today. His understanding of light and shading is also seen in the hatching and crosshatching techniques used in his drawings and etchings. Employing heavier and lighter hatching throughout the artwork creates the appearance of light and shadow quite effectively.

Delicious Detail

Rembrandt's full name is actually pretty long, but it wasn't always spelled the way it is today. He added the silent "d" to his name in 1633 by signing his work using the new spelling. No one knows why he began signing his work this way, but it has remained the proper spelling of his name ever since.

Monet Donut (1840–1926)

Claude Monet was a French Impressionist painter born in Paris, France in 1840. Monet was said to be a leader of Impressionism, a movement that focuses primarily on the effect of light and color on landscapes.

He began drawing at a very young age and even sold his first work, charcoal caricatures, at the age of 15. Later in life, he planted a huge garden and built a pond that he filled with water lilies imported from around the world. He spent the last 25 years of his life painting scenes from his garden, including his most famous series of water lilies.

Even though he is known for his beautiful landscapes, he didn't like the traditional approaches to landscape painting. He preferred to paint outdoors and observe the changes of light and color throughout the seasons. He would paint the same landscapes over and over again at different times. His technique involved using fast, broken brushstrokes of color in an effort to depict the perception of light. He also used the direction of these strokes to evoke feelings of either movement or stillness depending on how the strokes were oriented.

Delicious Detail

Monet was not just a painter but was also painted! Famous artist and friend of Monet, Pierre-Auguste Renoir, painted a portrait of Monet painting in his beloved garden in 1873.

Cassatt Donut (1844–1926)

Mary Cassatt was an American printmaker and painter who was born in Pennsylvania in 1844 but lived much of her adult life in France. She was a famed Impressionist who almost exclusively featured women in her work.

As a young girl, her father did not support her passion for art and refused to give her money for supplies. Her parents preferred that she get an education and prepare to be a wife and mother, but she was determined to follow her passion and eventually moved to Paris to pursue her painting.

She was very skilled at painting strict **value** ranges while also using a wide variety of pastel colors. Her soft, loose brushwork within a structured outline of her subject allowed her to **juxtapose** the softness of her most frequent subjects, children and mothers.

Delicious Detail

Cassatt was a strong believer in equality among the sexes and supported **women's suffrage**. She actually contributed 18 of her paintings to an exhibition in support of the movement. She was also a strong advocate for American museums and is credited with facilitating the donation of works that are still among the most popular paintings displayed to this day.

Van Gogh Donut (1853–1890)

Vincent van Gogh was born in Zundert, Netherlands in 1853. Although he wasn't recognized for his work during his lifetime (he only sold one piece while he was alive), his art has sold for record-breaking numbers in the years since his death. Since then he has cemented his place as one of the most recognized and appreciated Post-Impressionist artists.

Born as the eldest of six siblings, he was known to be quiet and reserved. He began studying art at the age of 16 but didn't begin working seriously as an artist until he was 27 years old. He was a very emotional artist, some people even considered him insane, and his intense emotions are apparent throughout his work.

Using a rich, striking color palette, he painted dramatically and energetically while using very small, short brushstrokes. These small strokes move across the canvas like schools of fish, creating larger swirling patterns throughout. This intense technique gives his paintings unparalleled movement and energy and would go on to heavily influence the Expressionist movement.

Delicious Detail

Although van Gogh only worked as an artist for about ten years, he produced more than 900 paintings and many drawings and sketches. It is estimated that, on average, throughout the time he was active, he created a new piece of art every day and a half!

Seurat Donut (1859–1891)

French painter Georges Seurat was born in 1859 in Paris, France. Due to an unknown illness, Seurat died early into his career and was only able to create seven full-size paintings. Even so, his work and legacy changed the art world. He is considered an icon of the nineteenth century, and his work ushered in a new era for **Neo-Impressionism**, a method that incorporates science and **color theory** to create beautiful art.

Born into a very wealthy family, he began taking art lessons from his uncle at a young age before going on to study art at the premier art school École des Beaux-Arts in Paris. After being turned away from one of the biggest exhibitions in Paris, the **Salon**, he decided to rebel and join other independent artists and went on to form the Société des Artistes Indépendants which is still active today.

He is famously known as the creator of **pointillism**, a method of painting that uses dots of pure color that seem to blend when viewed from a distance. In fact, he wouldn't blend any paints but instead would place various colored dots in close proximity to each other so that the eye would blend them. This incredibly inventive technique took a lot of effort. It is estimated that one of his most famous paintings has over 200,000 dots!

Delicious Detail

His invention of pointillism stemmed from ideas of color theory and optical illusion that scientists in Paris were advancing at the time. Just like many artists, such as da Vinci, have influenced science throughout history, it is also true that sometimes science will influence art!

MUCHA DONUT (1860–1939)

Alphonse Mucha was born in 1860 in what is now Czechia. His legacy as an **Art Nouveau** painter came from the commercial success of his posters and advertisements.

He grew up singing in the choir of his church, and maybe if things had been different, he would have chosen a career in singing. After a rejection from the Academy of Fine Arts, he entered the world of theater and began working at a Viennese theatrical design company where he designed stage sets, costumes, and posters.

Known as "le style Mucha," his style has a very distinct aesthetic because of its complexity and decoration. His ornate posters often feature his favorite subject, the "femme nouvelle," or the new woman. These ladies in beautiful pastel colors typically wore flowing robes, echoing the classic values of the Renaissance era, and are usually surrounded by the signature elements of his style, including decorative borders, intricate floral entanglements, and thick contour outlines. His inspiration and appreciation for plants and flowers can be seen in the complex overlapping vines and organic curves of his designs.

DELICIOUS DETAIL

Mucha's big break came when he created a poster for Sarah Bernhardt and her production of *Gismonda*. He was the only artist available at the time, which worked out for him because it jumpstarted his career practically overnight.

Klimt Donut (1862 – 1918)

World-famous Austrian painter Gustav Klimt was born near Vienna, Austria in 1862. Much of his work was influenced by the Symbolist movement as well as the decorative style of Art Nouveau.

Klimt was the second oldest of seven children, several of whom had artistic abilities. His father was a gold engraver, so he took an interest in precious metals from an early age.

His claim to fame came out of a period of his art called the golden phase. Many of his paintings from this period have gold leaf embedded in them, which is pure gold hammered into flat, thin sheets. In addition to utilizing mosaic techniques, he is also known for painting figures in a classical style, surrounded by highly ornamental and brilliantly composed areas of mixed media decoration.

Delicious Detail

Klimt wanted to make the subjects of his paintings feel like true royalty. You could even say he gave them the royal treatment by using materials like gold, silver, and other expensive metals in their portraits. Partly because of his use of fine metals, his paintings were very expensive for the time and remain some of the most expensive paintings in the world to this day.

MATISSE DONUT

(1869–1954)

Henri Matisse is considered by many to be the most important French painter of the nineteenth century. Born in 1869 in northern France, he would go on to lead the Fauvism movement.

He didn't start painting until his early twenties. He first studied law in Paris until he suddenly became ill. While recovering from his illness, his mother gave him paint supplies to help him pass the time. This time spent painting while on bed rest helped him decide his true passion was for art.

His painting style is characterized by visible brushstrokes of beautifully bright colors, and his work is full of these patches of color. Matisse didn't place too much importance on the realistic representation of his subject but instead focused on the use of color. His influence reached many other great painters including his longtime friend and art rival Pablo Picasso.

DELICIOUS DETAIL

As Matisse grew older and struggled to paint, he changed his approach to the cut-out technique. He would cut out shapes of paper and then arrange them using a stick in a process he called "painting with scissors."

PICASSO DONUT (1881 – 1973)

Pablo Picasso was born in 1881 in Málaga, Spain. He is known as the co-founder of **Cubism** and was the very first living artist to have his work **exhibited** at the Louvre.

He was already an artistic prodigy by the age of 15. Born as the son of a painter and art professor, he sold his first oil painting at the age of eight. He went on to study art at various schools before beginning a long and successful career as one of the most famous artists of his time.

His work changed and evolved throughout his career so much that it has been divided into periods; the most famous being Cubism. In Cubism, the subject of a painting is broken up into different and typically geometric forms. These forms are assembled in an **abstract** manner, often from various perspectives within the same painting.

DELICIOUS DETAIL

Picasso was once brought in for questioning by the police as an alleged art thief. His friend, Guillaume Apollinaire accused him of stealing Leonardo da Vinci's famed *Mona Lisa* from the Louvre. It was later discovered that a Louvre employee was actually to blame for the theft.

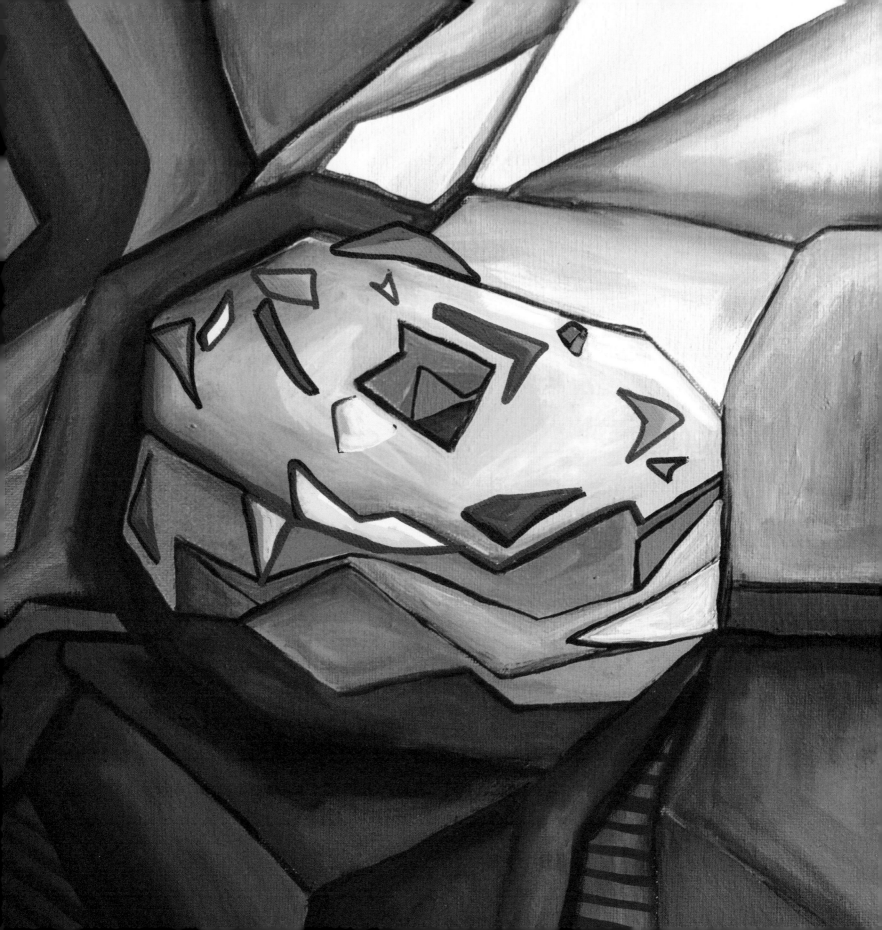

O'Keeffe Donut (1887–1986)

Georgia O'Keeffe was born in 1887 on a farm in Wisconsin. She greatly impacted modernism and made a name for herself with her famous paintings of skyscrapers and her unique depictions of flowers.

From a very young age, she was recognized as a talented painter. She received art lessons at home and went on to study art in Chicago and New York. She then worked as a commercial artist before teaching art and studying under artist Arthur Wesley Dow.

Her art took a lot of inspiration from the shapes and lines she saw in nature, specifically how those shapes changed as you zoomed in on them. Many of her paintings are done from a very close-up point of view which makes the subjects of the painting more abstract. She enjoyed experimenting with scale and painting things that were larger than life. She painted in very saturated, bright colors, using oil and watercolor paint primarily. Her style used curvy, rounded forms with lines that create areas of interesting negative space that abstract the shapes in her work even more.

Delicious Detail

O'Keeffe absolutely loved to drive in her Ford Model A. In fact, she loved the car so much that she transformed it into an art studio by customizing it so that the front seats could be removed, allowing her to work on her art right there in her car!

Dali Donut (1904 – 1989)

Salvador Dalí was born in Figueres, Spain in 1904. By the middle of the century, he was revered for his abstract artwork that expressed dreamlike interpretations of real-life objects.

He loved drawing from a young age and actually went to an art school when he was only 12. His parents were very supportive of his passion for art. His father even hosted a solo exhibition for him when he was 19. He later joined a group of artists in Paris where they created a new art movement called Surrealism.

Surrealist artists explore themes of imagination and abstraction with their art, blurring the line between what is and isn't real. Dalí's art style combines a sense of hyperrealism with its background landscapes and a sense of wonder through its vivid and unimaginable objects in the foreground. He hoped to challenge people's perceptions of reality and inspire a new sense of creativity.

Delicious Detail

One of Dalí's favorite motifs to hide in his paintings was an egg. The egg is meant to represent hope, love, and birth.

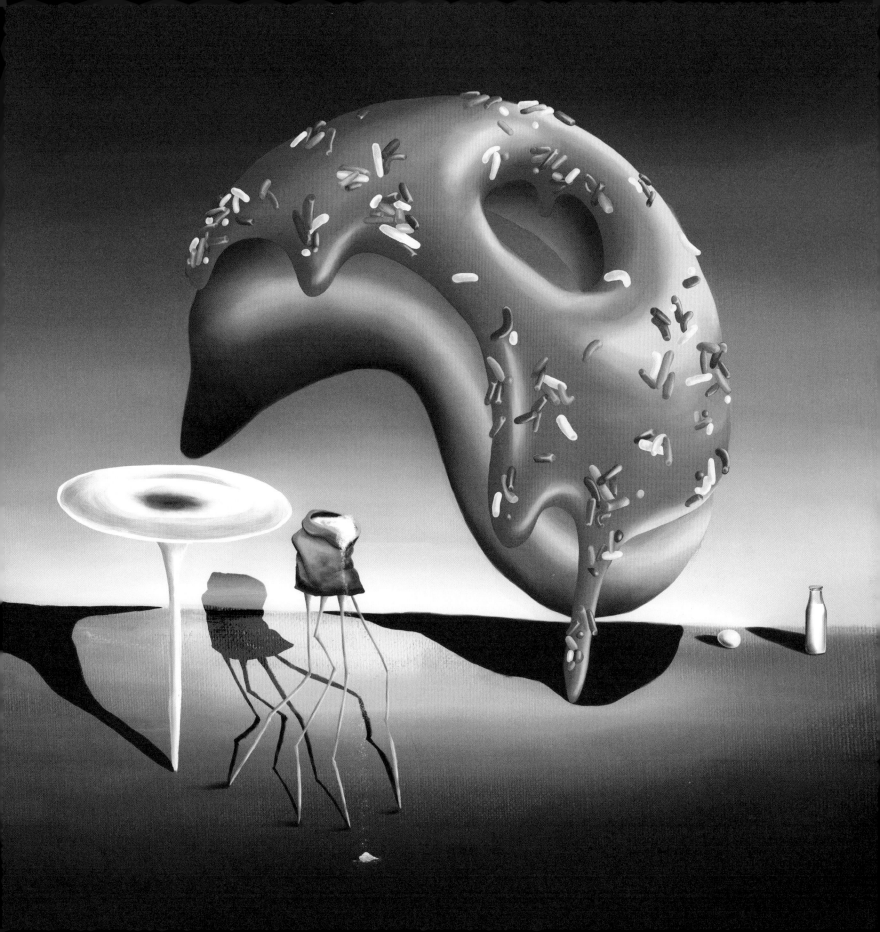

POLLOCK DONUT

(1912–1956)

American artist Paul Jackson Pollock was a leader in abstract expressionism. He was born in Wyoming in 1912. He became renowned for his unique drip technique.

Growing up, his family moved many times before they ended up in Los Angeles where he enrolled in art school. He eventually moved to New York City and worked maintenance at the Guggenheim museum, where he would later be granted his first solo exhibition.

His cutting-edge, large-scale painting technique involved laying canvas flat on the ground and applying paint by splashing, pouring, or drizzling it. He did not worry about the outcome of a painting, preferring to let it to take on a life of its own. He found the significance of his artwork was in the physical act of creating it rather than in the final painting itself.

DELICIOUS DETAIL

Pollock began to label many of his famous works using numbers rather than titles. He didn't want anyone viewing his work to be distracted by the name or to attribute meaning to the painting because of the name. Even more unique, the numbers he chose weren't even in order!

YOKOO DONUT

(1936–present)

Born in Nishiwaki, Japan in 1936, Tadanori Yokoo loved to draw as a child and, perhaps as a result, would grow up to become Japan's most famous **Pop Artist** of the modern era.

As a graphic designer, Yokoo went against the current in Tokyo in the 1960s and 1970s, where modernism and simplicity were center stage. He became regarded as an anti-modernist artist. His colorful **psychedelic** aesthetic and style allowed him to thrive in the **avant-garde** scene and gain major status overseas, where he was the first ever graphic designer to get a solo exhibition at New York's MoMA (Museum of Modern Art).

Influenced by Pop Art, Japanese culture, Surrealism, and **Ukiyo-e prints**, his unique artistic style represents Japanese culture of the time. In Yokoo's mind, colors are directly connected to memories and emotions from his childhood, and from that he creates art. He was obsessed with including popular icons from his childhood into his work, such as Japanese playing cards, picture-story shows, match labels, as well as American Pop Art images. Yokoo's vivid collages full of Japanese imagery came together to create a very original, psychedelic style that bursts with color and communicates thought-provoking ideas.

Delicious Detail

His art influenced the psychedelic movement in the US and has appeared on album covers and concert posters for some of the most legendary names in music history, including The Beatles, Miles Davis, Santana, and many more!

BASQUIAT DONUT (1960–1988)

Jean-Michel Basquiat was born in New York in 1960. He would go on to become a prominent artist in the 1980s even though he was only in his twenties.

Born to a Haitian father and Puerto Rican mother, he could speak French, Spanish, and English and was a poet and musician in addition to being a visual artist. At age 17, he dropped out of school and began making street art and graffiti. Under the tag SAMO, he created art on the streets and subways around Brooklyn and the Bronx and began gaining notoriety for his work.

Coming from a background as a street artist, Basquiat was masterful at using mixed media surfaces and materials to create his wild paintings. He enjoyed experimenting, often mixing graffiti with his own writings and poetry. His work features symbols, such as crowns and arrows, as well as figures from African, American, and Latin cultures. His art often focused on poverty versus wealth, race segregation, and other social issues.

DELICIOUS DETAIL

Basquiat not only created incredible graffiti art and paintings, he was also part of the music scene. As a musician, he formed a band and produced a rap album for which he made the album artwork. Possibly due to its obscurity, but certainly due its cover art, a copy of the record sold at auction for over $100,000!

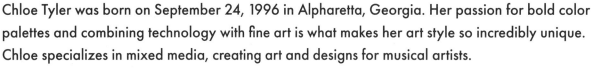

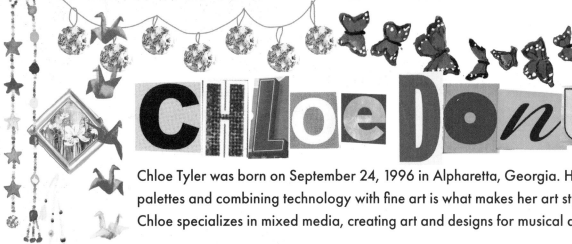

CHLoe DOnUT (1996–present)

Chloe Tyler was born on September 24, 1996 in Alpharetta, Georgia. Her passion for bold color palettes and combining technology with fine art is what makes her art style so incredibly unique. Chloe specializes in mixed media, creating art and designs for musical artists.

Her love for art began when she was in high school. Her mother supported her passion from the very beginning and encouraged her to express herself through her art and beyond. She even allowed Chloe to paint a mural on the back of her bedroom door which she later helped take off its hinges and carry into Chloe's AP Art Class. From helping herself to the art supplies in Mrs. Pickens's off-limits storage closet in high school to learning how to incorporate technology into her work from her Advanced Illustration professor Mr. Murawski, her bright career as an artist and graphic designer has only just begun.

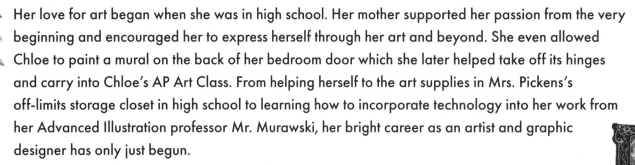

Since the day she picked up a paintbrush, she has experimented with a variety of mediums and techniques within graphic design and fine arts. She believes that graphic design should be approached with a certain stubbornness and that artists shouldn't venture too far from fine art. That belief has pushed her into a world of endless creative opportunities. While she is still working to find her voice as an artist, bold and intense color are consistent throughout her body of work. Her goal is to create art that forces people to take notice.

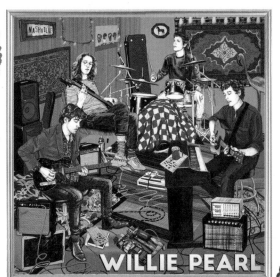

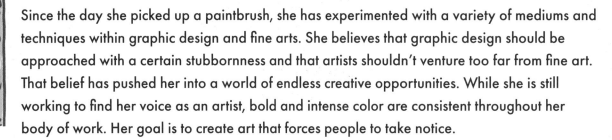

DELiCiOU$ DETaiL

Chloe rarely ever paints self-portraits, but in this painting, she found that she wanted to focus on her creative space, a place where she says she feels most vulnerable and able to express her emotions. Her space reflects her identity and her mindset in that there is always a lot going on at any given time.

Tips & Tricks for TASTY TECHNIQUE

An insight into the recipes for the perfect donuts!

Rembrandt's famous shadows are achieved by crosshatching your strokes. The more you crosshatch strokes in a specific area, the darker your value will become.

Draw a donut, cut it up into triangles, and then piece it back together! That is a technique Picasso used to practice when planning his painting.

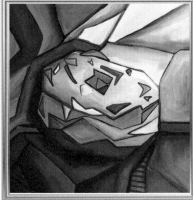

Picasso

Rembrandt

To achieve Seurat-style pointillism, it's easiest to start with a contour outline of your shape in a darker color and then add the rest of the dots on top.

For Monet, the alternating placement of vertical and horizontal lines on the water are meant to emulate the reflections and refractions of light on the water.

Seurat

Monet

Mucha

Use as many organic entanglements as you can to mimic Mucha's decorative style. Sketch it out in pencil first and make sure you have a good eraser!

Make sure you paint each brushstroke in the same direction in order to imitate van Gogh's fluidity of movement.

van Gogh

Klimt

Try incorporating materials like aluminum foil into your work to mimic Klimt's use of metals!

Dalí

If you want to be like Dalí, you gotta be wacky. Next time you wake up after having a crazy dream, do a quick sketch of it and make your dream the subject of your next painting!

Matisse

To paint like Matisse, sketch a contour outline of your subject, then loosen your hands and paint freely within those lines! Use whatever bright colors catch your eye—there are no rules!

Yokoo

Yokoo features pop culture in his work, so include some of your favorite popular icons.

O'Keeffe

Get up close and personal with your subject to discover new angles and curves like O'Keeffe!

da Vinci

To give your illustration that similarly aged look of a da Vinci sketch, try using coffee grounds mixed in hot water to stain your paper before drawing on it. Or use the coffee stain as a watercolor wash to give some shadow to your drawing.

When imitating Basquiat, keep piling on those layers! Allow the paint to dry for a little bit in between layers to make sure your bold colors don't mix too much.

Basquiat

To achieve that soft, creamy look that Cassatt is famous for, don't be afraid to get your hands dirty. Your fingertips are the best tools for blending pastels!

Apply your liquid paint with sticks and branches to practice the drip technique Pollock was renowned for! Make sure to use paint that can pour, like house paint!

Cassatt

Pollock

Having trouble mimicking the Renaissance-era cracked paint look of Michelangelo? Try priming your canvas with a coat of crackle paint! It will gently crack the surface as your painting dries.

Michelangelo

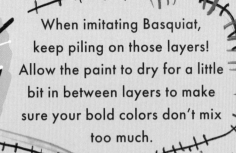
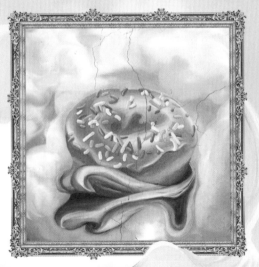

GLOSSARY

Abstract
Expressing feelings of a particular idea without providing a concrete image

Abstract expressionism
An art movement beginning in the mid-twentieth century with an emphasis on spontaneity

Apprentice
A person who works under a mentor in order to learn

Art Nouveau
An art style that was defined by its use of dynamic curves and its highlighting of natural body shapes

Avant-garde
Describes an unusual, new, or experimental idea

Caricature
A piece of art that depicts a person with exaggerated details

Charcoal
A piece of black carbon that is used to create the color black in various ways in various artforms

Chiaroscuro
The practice of arranging light and dark parts in a work of art in a harmonious way

Classical style
To do something with old, uncommon techniques or in a way that evokes a feeling of the past

Color theory
Established methods that utilize different colors to complement one another

Commercial artist
Artist who creates art used to advertise a product or service

Crosshatching
A form of shading produced by crossing lines over one another

Cubism
An avant-garde art movement that utilized the restructuring of sharp objects to produce abstract art

Cut-out technique
A method used by Henri Matisse near the end of his career in which he cut pieces of paper with scissors and combined them to make art

Draftsman
A person who draws sketches of machinery and structures

Drip technique

A technique used by Jackson Pollock in which he would drip paint onto a canvas to create an abstract work of art

Dutch Golden Age

An art movement in the Netherlands with an emphasis on still lifes

E

Etching

A design made by removing pieces of metal with acid to replicate another design

Exhibit

To showcase one's art in a communal space

Expressionist movement

An art movement that sought to create art based on emotions and moods, rather than facts or reality

F

Fauvism movement

An art movement that highlighted bold colors instead of natural shades

Foreground

The part of a painting that is closest to the viewer

Fresco

A painting made on fresh plaster before the plaster dries

G

Golden phase

A time during Gustav Klimt's career when much of his art included pieces of gold

H

Hatching

A form of shading produced by drawing lines parallel to one another

Hyperrealism

An art style that depicts its subject in an extremely realistic manner, to the point of almost seeming real

Impressionism

An art movement that utilized small brushstrokes to emphasize the effects of color and light

J

Juxtapose

To place an object close to another, often to encourage comparison

L

Landscape

A piece of art that depicts a piece of land or sea in a way that highlights nature

M

Marble

A type of limestone used to make sculptures

Miller

A person who tends a flour mill

Mirror writing

A method of writing text backwards so it can only be read by looking at it in a mirror

Modernism

An art movement with the goal to move past previous art traditions to create something entirely new

Mosaic technique

A technique that involves various colors or materials coming together to form a new image

Motif

An aspect of a piece of art that is referenced multiple times or expresses the theme of a work

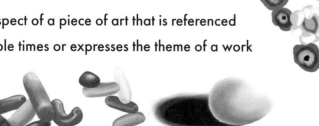

N

Negative space

The blank space around a subject in a piece of art that helps highlight the subject and the blank space at the same time, or create an optical illusion

Neo-Impressionism

An art movement from the late nineteenth century started by Georges Seurat which continued the artistry of Impressionism and focused on using bright colors

P

Palette

A range of colors used by an artist

Period

A division of time that often has significant moments associated with it

Pointillism

The practice of creating art by placing tiny dots of pure color close to one another so that they seem connected to the viewer's eye

Pop Artist

An artist that bases their work on modern pop culture and media

Portrait

A work of art that portrays the likeness of a person

Post-Impressionism

An art movement that was started in response to Impressionism, going against the notions of natural color and light

Psychedelic

An art style using bright colors and abstract patterns

R

Rembrandt lighting

A technique created by Rembrandt used to achieve portrait lighting with minimal equipment

Renaissance

An art movement that occurred in Europe, more specifically Italy, during the fifteenth century that represented a time of "rebirth"

S

Salon

An art exhibition in Paris which showcased many incredible artists

Self-portrait

A work of art that portrays the likeness of oneself

Studio

The working room of an artist

Surrealism

An avant-garde art movement associated with art that sought to inspire and influence unconscious parts of the mind

Symbolist movement

An art movement that focused on the use of metaphors and other symbols

U

Ukiyo-e print

A type of art from the Edo period of Japan that showcased life in Japan in the form of paintings and woodblock prints

V

Value

How light or dark a color is

W

Women's suffrage

A feminist movement in which women worked to gain the right to vote in various parts of the world

Scan this code for more fun ideas and information to explore the world of art.

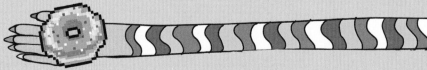

47

Go get your hands messy.

-Chloe